Double Jinx

Double Jinx
poems

Nancy Reddy

milkweed
editions

Published 2015 by Milkweed Editions
Printed in the United States of America
Cover design by Adam B. Bohannon
Author photo by Cynthia Marie Hoffman
Interior design by Adam B. Bohannon
The text of this book is set in Perpatua.
15 16 17 18 19   5 4 3 2 1
First Edition

Milkweed Editions, an independent nonprofit publisher, gratefully acknowledges sustaining support from the the Lindquist & Vennum Foundation; the McKnight Foundation; the National Endowment for the Arts; the Target Foundation; and other generous contributions from foundations, corporations, and individuals. Also, this activity is made possible by the voters of Minnesota through a Minnesota State Arts Board Operating Support grant, thanks to a legislative appropriation from the arts and cultural heritage fund, and a grant from the Wells Fargo Foundation Minnesota. For a full listing of Milkweed Editions supporters, please visit www.milkweed.org.

LIBRARY OF CONGRESS CATALOGING-IN-PUBLICATION DATA
Reddy, Nancy, 1982-
[Poems. Selections]
Double Jinx / Nancy Reddy. — First edition.
pages cm
ISBN 978-1-57131-477-2 (alk. paper) — ISBN 978-1-57131-938-8 (ebook)
I. Title.
PS3618.E4269A6 2015
811'.6—dc23
2014050288

MILKWEED EDITIONS is committed to ecological stewardship. We strive to align our book production practices with this principle, and to reduce the impact of our operations in the environment. We are a member of the Green Press Initiative, a nonprofit coalition of publishers, manufacturers, and authors working to protect the world's endangered forests and conserve natural resources. Double Jinx was printed on acid-free 30% postconsumer-waste paper by Versa Press.

for Smith

CONTENTS

1

Ex Machina

The chorus girls descend, their wings a wonder
      of feather and zipline. The oboes
   in the orchestra pit yawn
as if to gulp them whole, but the girls
      are singing and so swallow down

   their fear. The villain shows himself
too soon and is all wrong for this play—
      not a dashing captain but a pirate
   with a stick shift for an arm and a stopwatch
in his heart. Where the audience

should be—the rows of lovely velvet seats
      and numbered placards, donated
   by the dead or named for them—there's
only sea. The violinists do a kick turn
      and set out into the waves. What happened

   to the playwright, to the plot? Who will stitch
the chorus to the theme? Who will,
      when the curtain drops, unhook the beauties
   from their wings and turn them back
to girls, wrap terrycloth robes around

their sequined bodysuits? We cannot wait
      for angels. We'll be our own gods now.
   Watch us swinging from the rafters
like a lifeboat or a bird of prey.

Divine and Mechanical Bodies

The year my sister turned into a crow
  I ran the cinder track around the football field for hours. I stayed on
after practice ended, after coach packed up

his whistle and his stopwatch, after the other girls changed back
  into sweats and carpooled home. At my house

  my sister gathered all the shiny things. She plucked the buttons
from our parkas and strung them from the bedposts,
lined the closet doors with tinfoil and propped the silver-plated serving trays
  along the dressers so that everywhere she looked

she'd see her own eyes looking back. She wouldn't speak.

  When our mother called us down to dinner
she answered with a raucous preening call, she piled mall kiosk pendants
      around her feathered neck. She wouldn't eat

the meals our mother cooked and instead slurped juice from cans, clawed
  the soft and flaky centers from the caramels

in the cut-glass candy dish our mother kept for guests. She grew
bird-boned and slender, a brittle core inside each inky feather. That year,
  though no one had died, not really,

my mother filled the basement freezer with casseroles,
  each aluminum dish an archaeological dig of hash browns, beef tips
browned in butter, cream of something soup. In bio lab

we pinned and bisected earthworms, diagrammed their tiny hearts
    on worksheets. Somewhere a teacher called out *kingdom, phylum, family*.

    We smeared the cultured cells from petri dishes onto slides and marveled
at their manufactured one-cell lives. I ran the track each afternoon,
        my mix tape turned up loud. The sun set

earlier and earlier each day behind the goal posts. At home
my mother diced and browned the onions. My sister

    made herself a feather bed. The first snow fell around us as we slept,
flakes soft as down, clotting the trees whose leaves had not yet
    turned and fallen, turning the lawn
bright as a spotlight.

The Case of the Double Jinx

THE SCARLET SLIPPER MYSTERY

You're Nancy Drew and you drive a blue coupe.
You drive fast. Your mother is dead.
She's the new-hired help and you're a nosy houseguest.
She's a model turned jewel thief and you're hot
on her trail. She's a pretender to the fortune
of the county's richest missing bachelor.
You're solving mysteries that stump the cops.
You sass them back. You're flip-haired and eagle-eyed.
You're a daredevil detective on the trail of a breathtaking
escape. She fooled you once and won't again.

THE FOOTPRINTS IN THE FLOWERBEDS

You're peering in her windows. You're watching
as she hides the proof beneath the sink,
as she scrubs her hands with lye. She splashes bleach
across the tile. You're watching as she runs
the bath. You watch. She's wasp-waisted
and flaxen-haired. You're not the better sister.
You're no one's good-time gal. You're a bayou,
a river caught fire. You're armed with flashlight
and revolver. You're casing the estate.
Ned will get you for your date at four. He's late.

THE MYSTERY OF THE WOODEN LADY

She's a cocktail dress and you're day-old rye.
You find a blond hair on the sofa bed,
stockings in the spare room. You come home late
one night and find your house lit like a birthday.
You tiptoe to the window, your skirt's hem

catching on the hedges. She's in your house.
She's dancing slow with fickle Ned. She laughs
at all his jokes. Now you're a pincushion.
You're the sulfur smell of rotten eggs. You do
the only thing you can. You run.

THE CLUE IN THE BREAKFAST NOOK

You run home to River Heights. You bolt the door.
You're a sure shot, an expert swimmer,
a gourmet cook. You bake birthday cakes
and ice them all with arsenic. You learn to knit.
You believe in the jinx. You won't say his name,
won't look at the phone. She's a damsel
in dishwashing gloves. She's at your kitchen table,
sugaring her tea. Ned's a lost sock.
She smiles your smile and wears his jacket.
She hums. You're gimlet-eyed. You're losing steam.

THE SECRET LOST AT SEA

This time you're the belle of Miami Beach.
You're busting up a gang of smugglers.
You drink rum and dance all night. You learn
to surf. A strange man licks the saltwater
from your hair. The smugglers are setting sail
for Cuba. You're an inside job. You're on their tail.
There's a girl here dressed as you. You surprise her
on the ship's back stairs. Now the jig is up.
You're found out, tied up, left to drown.
You tapdance SOS against the cabin's roof.

THE CASE OF THE DISAPPEARING HUSBANDS

You're on vacation in the snow-stunned Alps
when the innkeeper comes to you for help.
He's getting threats from a dark-wigged woman
who claims that she's your twin. You're snowed in.
He tells you all the town's most handsome men
go missing after dark. You wear a borrowed mink
and sleuth by candlelight. You smell Ned's soap.
She's a false wall. She's a trap door. You're dangling
from the rafters. Ned's tied up in the basement.
He's bound and gagged. He's never been so grateful.

THE STRANGE MESSAGE ON THE TRAILHEAD

You get him back but he won't stay.
Silly Ned, he wanders off. He's lost
in state parks, disappears on dinner dates.
You're on the case. He's lucky. You rescue him,
time and time again. You get him back
in pieces. You swear you hear his voice
before the dial tone clicks on. You find
his toenail clippings on the tile. His name's
a rock you rub against your teeth.
He's a wishbone saved beside the kitchen sink.

THE INVISIBLE INTRUDER

You're digging through her trashcan. You're watching
as she slips the proof beneath her skin.
Her body now the briefcase full of unmarked bills.
She scrapes her palms against the wall's fresh paint.
She swings a bag of bones into the yard.
Her hands flush red and you know you'll never
see that boy again. Born different

you could have been sisters. Like those butterflies
in shadowboxes, pinned and mounted above the mantle.
Now you're the double agent. You're calling all the shots.

THE GIRL WHO COULDN'T REMEMBER
You're creeping through her flowerbeds.
There's no crime to detect here but your own
and Ned's long gone. You're the back door's loose latch,
the spare key beneath the mat. You're pawing
through her dresses, pirouetting in her heels.
She's in your town now. You're in her hair.
One quick slit and you're in the space inside
her skin. You hold your breath then whisper.
You thumb the ligaments. You kick the tires.
You loved that dumb boy, too. Before he died.

THE TRIPLE HOAX
She's a foxtrot. She's a jinx and you can't speak.
You're a dahlia and she's the state fair's
bright-eyed Susans. Or she's the real Nancy
and you're a costume party. Didn't you feel
made of paper? Didn't you hide for years
from houses, the streets of windows
that left you feeling skinned and eyed? Even
the neighbor's house for sale, the mulch and rows
of transplant tulips, their faces open—
how their black stamens stared and stripped you bare.

Understudy

When the curtain splits, the stage contains a single singing woman.
    She hits the final crystal goblet high note
on her solo and then sheds a cinematic tear. She's bathed
    in stardust and applause. You're the other

    woman, stranded just offstage,
mouthing words you've learned
    by heart. At dress rehearsal you were costumed
as your better self. Now she's the critics' darling and you're

a cast-off prop. Darling, you're an asterisk
    in the program's slick pages. You study
her body. Learn the way when striding to her mark
    she leads with her hips, how beneath the flood lights

    her slender shinbones flash like knives. Her clavicle's a coat hook
in the Act II strapless gown and so you fast until your shoulder blades
    float up from your spine. You file your nails
until like hers they're perfect crescent moons. At the encore she's a streetlamp

gathering moths but in her dressing room
    she dozes after a sold-out matinee, pancake foundation
smudged across her satin pillowcase. You smear her beauty cream
    beneath your eyes. You lean into the mirror at her vanity

    and paint your mouth to match her practiced pout. Watch
the unplucked fuzz above her upper lip
    as she exhales in sleep. Match your breath to hers.
Hum the closing notes.

Possible and Impossible Sentences

The girls all breathe together. Teacher in her grey wool dress
	clicks up and down the rows, her ruler counting time
across her palm. The girls take down in ink her every word,
	each one writing a synchronized script so finely tuned
that even the girls' own mothers cannot tell apart
	their cursive hands. A rich-grammared language like Latin
needs armchairs and lullabies to soothe it to sleep
	but gets instead these girls with notebooks and manuals
of grammar, the chapters thick with case and tense
	and mood. The younger girls copy out the verbs:
amo, amas, amat, their little hearts twitching
	through the subject endings. One girl reads
a frightening scene from Ovid where a fleeing girl
	becomes a tree and she can't help but shudder, the thought
of being left there by the creekbed and always
	there for touching. She counts down through her dress
the rows of ribs that keep her bound together, she knows
	below the bark and tendon lies the spalting at the core of her
that makes for fine-grained lumber.

Little, Red

As a girl she gorged on words. She swallowed up
the grainy yellow paperback the housekeeper slipped behind the sofa,
    the newspaper clippings that greeted her each morning

at breakfast with her eggs. She walked for days inside the gilt-edged forests
    of the storybooks Father presented her each time he returned
from whatever elsewhere swallowed him from time to time. Her ribcage

    was papered with fables, her sternum sheaved with verse
and *ever after*, belly plump with rising action. Roads, she'd learned,
    could not be trusted. Where, for example,

was Mother? What road had gobbled her
    the day she set down the path with Father's billfold
to buy the Sunday roast and did not come back? Better to stay inside

    with chapter books and tea, the fire cracking consolingly. In books,
fires were emergency or escape hatch. Wet wood would smoke
    and were she stranded on a desert island she'd simply gather kindling

and wait for an airplane to swoop down in rescue. Here, the fires were ordinary
    and not quite warm enough, lit with pine trees the woodsman chopped
and laid neatly on the hearth. Where, she wondered,

    was the woodsman? She hadn't seen his mustached face, his ax
in ages. And even in the quiet castle
    she was never lonely, not with grandma's smile

framed above the mantle, the carnivorous rumbling from the bookshelves.
Sometimes she heard a distant howling but mostly she slept soundly
and woke with fur beside her on the pillow. One night

she found a hidden *Grey's Anatomy*
and saw the girl pinned to the page in vivisection. Could she
be pink inside like that? No decent girl

would go around the world uncooked. Girls, she saw,
were caverns. Better to be a forest instead. The last fall leaves
are falling on the well-trod path, the wolf inside her

making his way to the cabin and the garden.

Girl-Terrarium

The girl beneath the glass
liked it. Her world was very small
and still and smelled only
of the forsythia blossoms she'd gathered
that morning, just before the armed guards
put her under. Beneath the glass
she didn't have a body, so she became
a plant instead. In fall
her pale arms turned to birch bark,
flaking and delicate, and come first frost
she was a holly bush, her mouth
a wreath of stiff and glossy leaves
studded with berries. Her torso stayed flesh
and her nightdress rose to meet the glass
when she exhaled. In spring she was
a hedgerow of honeysuckle, a blooming earth
that no one else could touch. The guards
came back, though in the end no prince
would have a girl half-tree. The king's man
came and roused her with his tongue
between her teeth.

Lucy in Chrysalis

One year every girl in town smelled sweet
with blood. That was the year you rode your high horse
to the corner store, the year you fell in love

with the sentence, how the thrust and stumble
of syntax always makes good its promises.
You spend lunchtime on the schoolyard

digging worms and blessing each one
before tossing their mulchy bodies skyward.
In the lunchroom the other girls purse

their glossed lips and clear the table. Now
it's your birthday. The sliced cake sweats grease
in the backyard. Soda fizzles in Dixie cup rows.

The other girls whisper and giggle, won't sing, won't
eat. The rented magician's jokes go flat and worst of all,
your chest is flat, though the big girls told you

that when you finally passed the pencil test
they'd take you to the Bon-Ton to buy a real
bra with white lace and a front clasp for when the boys

snap, and you try it, but your row of sharpened No. 2s
clatter to the tile one by one. You decide you're sick
of being a girl. You've read the books and know

the time has passed for your discovery as a caterpillar
or a Cinderella. You ride your bike to town
and beg the wandering saints summering

in the town square's gazebo to take them with you
when the flock flies south for winter. You're done
being the girl left holding the tincan telephone's slack end.

You'd rather be a hayfield or a hatpin. You thought
by now you'd be a grocer or an acrobat.

Big Valley's Last Surviving Beauty Queen

Once you were a pretty thing, quick-witted
as a mousetrap. Your ponytail was slick like horse hair.
    One word-poor schoolboy said so. He meant well,
anyway. The boys all did, and they lined the butcher's alley every Thursday

    to carry home your brisket and your cold cuts. You loved them all then,
for a moment, and kissed each one behind the Dairy Queen
    to prove it. Only the milkman failed to love you back.
No matter. You wore a peach print apron
        over your second-best dress. Saturdays were dancing days

but no one ever asked you, not even in your pinkest party dress.
    The boys danced slow with other girls, your homely cousins
and your classmates, even a ham-hocked former tennis partner.
    They polkaed and they pinwheeled. You stared
into your punch. You were once

    a pretty thing. All the town men said so. One said *pretty as a picture*
and then you were a picture. They hung you on the wall. You shook a little,
        looked at. The town council gathered in the mayor's foyer
to catcall at your profile. They lit you with an oil lamp

    so the town could look on you all night.
They framed you in the square between the gazebo
        and the war memorial. They ran you through the mimeograph
and handed out the copies after graduation mass. They made you into
        a filmstrip and all the children clapped, your image lightbulb-thinned,

blinking as the projector flapped. The wives cooked chicken breasts
and gravy from a packet, potatoes au gratin from a box. The men hid you
in their TV rooms. They drank canned beer
and during each commercial put the sound on mute
and stroked your inky purple hair.

Cinderella Story

The stepsisters weren't jealous
exactly. They knew that what they lacked in poise or beauty
        they made up with certain other

advantages. Though their dishwater tresses would never
        turn a prince's fickle head
they had instead golf privileges at the kingdom's

        most exclusive clubs, a chit to which they signed
their dear departed daddy's name as they ordered bottle after bottle
        of the best champagne. What looks they had

could be kept up or improved on altogether
        with tiny pricey jars of night cream and visits
to the surgeon. And didn't they deserve it,

        had they not earned their fortune—
all those years of *yes sir* and *of course daddy*, all the years
        they'd had to pull their pretty sister's hair in secret

lest she cry and they be spanked or sent
        away from supper hungry. And when for one brief season
the prince turned his favor on her

        they knew it wouldn't last. He had dresses made
to suit her slender yet full-bosomed figure, he sent
        a golden coach to fetch her for moonlight after-dinner dancing

and they knew she'd be a night-time princess
        only. They found her morning-after on the cobblestones,
coach and driver vanished, her dress turned back to tatters.

Before the Catalog of Boats

Every year they cut the cake together,
their twinned arms becoming one hand

on the knife, the jelly filling cadaverous
between layers of white box cake. Asleep,

you couldn't tell the girls apart, Helen nestled
against the other sister like a teaspoon

in the kitchen drawer. In Math they counted out
the times together and in Home Ec they cut

tote bags and circle skirts from the same cloth. But one day
Helen's sudden beauty flared up like a brand.

Boys came calling, but her father
wouldn't look at her, not even when she soloed

at the Easter Mass, not even when as Harvest Queen
she wore a beaded gown and waved beside her date,

a boy slack-jawed with her beauty and his luck,
as they looped the track in the shop teacher's

borrowed truck. *Where had this girl come from?*
and her parents wondered, too. Even as the sisters

hung their graduation tassels
from their Chrysler's rearview mirror, Helen always knew

her real life waited elsewhere. She sometimes wondered—
her father in the sky, the man with masks and feathers

does he watch her ever? Had she been a man
she could have gone to find that father. The pretty sister

finds a prince and goes to war. The other sister
stays home and simmers.

Why the McKean County Lifeguards Left Town

Because our mothers taught the swan dive and the snap of swim cap,
       the flip turn, its whoosh and kick in deep end. Because
we learned the butterfly when our suits filled out and our shoulders
          grew strong but we loved best the weeks at Lake Chautauqua,
our mothers drinking gin and gossiping in espadrilles and party dresses,
      our fathers grilling store-bought patties to a crisp.
When a girl went out into the water there, you couldn't say for certain

what would seize her. We lifeguarded that whole summer
         at the reservoir and while the toddlers flapped in water wings,
      while the pre-teens called out *Marco*—
Polo, flopping and kicking in the drinking water damned to serve the three
   surrounding counties, while no one ever drowned
we practiced our heimlichs and our mouth to mouth. We weren't

         the prettiest girls and we weren't the smartest. We knew
how to haul a body from the water, when to throw a life vest and when
     to leave the boy for dead. We sunned ourselves on beaches made
        of trucked-in sand, the same stuff filling playground sandboxes
   in all the villages around. We believed in the elegant escape

and so we packed our swim trunks, our beach towels and our novels.
   We gassed up our cars and hightailed it for the coast. Before our mothers
could call us to our dinner tables, we sped off down the forest highway —
     its logging trucks, its bait and beer shops, already going out of season.

Paper Anniversary

The happy couple's in the kitchen
so I'm in the side yard doing my best imitation
of a doghouse. Inside, the wife pops champagne
and pours it in the bridal flutes while the husband
hand washes the china. He's cooked her coq au vin.
The leftovers cool in the weighty Dutch oven
a distant aunt ordered off the registry. The wife unwraps
a novel bookmarked with a plane ticket from the last trip
they took apart. They take the year-old top tier, weeping,
from its corner of the freezer. He carves a slice
and places an iced rosette inside her open mouth. Outside,
frost grips the windows. The gift wrap flares
a toxic orange in the hearth. I'm an outbuilding.
My shingles won't stick and my foundation's made of sod.
The wife is loved. She gets to sleep inside the house.

A Theory of Disaster

We thought we'd passed into
the *after*. Like firefighters who can't outrun the wildfire
and instead shelter under blankets, breathing earth
until the fire either takes them or passes over, leaving them unharmed,

we craved the clarity of disaster, the bracing cleave
of before and after. It hurt like that, at least, limbs
wrenched from sockets, like the baby girl
born loose-limbed, her hips dislocated so that on the exam table

she lay like spatchcocked chicken. We'd thought our pain
would be simple and locatable. We pushpinned all the parts that hurt
and gave each one a name. I thought of *after* as a wolf
and I waited for its jaws.

2

My Girlhood Apothecary

It hurt at first, having a body. My new skin itching
like an opened wound, like the daylilies splitting

the soil beside the shed. Now I lay each morning
beneath this moth-pocked canopy. I remember Father

in his milk truck, Mother in the hen house, spilling grain
and pocketing eggs. Inside the nursery, kittens

stalked the babies sleeping in their bassinets. That house
was where I learned to name the world

correctly. Learned *lobelia, chrysanthemum, narcissus,
forsythia*. Which flowers poison and which

to use for garnish. I learned that when I loved you
I didn't need to eat. Spent one year there

a hysterical mute. So tell me again how for years all I did
was disappoint. Tell me again—I dare you, sweet—that she's

the one who loves you better. Each time I travel back to you
your cheeks are thinner, your touch more brittle.

Genealogy

My father's mother was a jewel box. Her heart
was charmed enamel. She wore it on a pendant
and it nestled in her throat's hot hollow.
    They bundled in for winter.

She wrapped the boys in rugs and propped them up
before the fire. They watched the lake
freeze over, the aphid-bitten roses
    glazed again in ice.

The fire spit and roared. She passed her heart
between her palms. She held her heart
between her teeth, the display case
    of her open jaws.

Family Portrait with Rosary and Steak Knife

Because they did not then have men,
my mother and her sister gave their girls a childhood
of artichokes with béarnaise, eggs benedict

on Sundays after mass. And once, live and snapping lobsters
from the Italian grocer in the Strip.
Married young inside the Church

and divorced back out a decade later,
they were moored pewside through communion
because they would not confess themselves

adulteresses weekly. They watched
their daughters waiting single file
to take Christ's body

on their tongues. My mother
plunged her mother's good Case knife,
a wedding gift, into each lobster's back

and sent it shrieking
to the pot. My sister wouldn't eat
but saved the shell,

scalded red. She hid its burnished husk
beneath her bed and took it out at night
to speak to it. She wagged

its jagged sawtooth claws,
its blackened gumdrop eyes.
She made it answer back.

Genealogy

My father was a wolf.

Portrait of my Father
as a Young Man with a Bludgeon

For a year my father beat anything that moved
or looked his way. After a narrow miss of Vietnam,
after months in Nevada testing bombs, after
an Army base in Germany and language school
where he learned to pass for Dutch, after his mother's
drowned-liver death as he flew across the Atlantic,
after his father's mistress moved in and tore
his mother's furs to shreds, after his first love
got married in a bowling alley,

he drove home to Philadelphia. He found the fountain black
and glistening with algal scum and rot, the mortar
on the front steps chipped and gray.
His father's set-adrift and aimless cruelty
crackled in that house like ice in Scotch.
That year my father beat his black heart clean.

In Language School My Father Learns
to Pass for Dutch

He stands before the mirror and wraps his mouth
and tongue around umlauts and diphthongs. Beneath
the mustache he grew to mark his discharge
his lips form foreign sounds. A copper penny

in his mouth, a bit he can't quite close
his lips around. He learns to slice the air
between words, to hold the long vowels
longer, a fresh egg between his teeth. He'd learned

to love liverwurst and spread it thick
on pumpernickel or marbled rye. He'll never be
quite native. He dreams at last in German,
and speaking in his sleep the words

are first strangled, their consonants too thick
for his American tongue. Then they're a stream.

My Father Flying Home From War, 1975

Because her dying is slow, he's waited months to ask for leave
and board this plane. Frankfurt, first, then London, where he'd changed
into civilian clothes, the button-down and Levi's his father hates,
and now, contained in the recirculating oxygen and polyester seating
of the economy cabin, he presses his wrists against the rivets,

raising welts. She's not dead yet. Or if she is, there's no way to know,
held high above the Atlantic while his mother's a web of IVs
at home in Philadelphia. She loved all creatures, even crows, and labored hard
at drinking herself to death. In the long years of her dying,
one president was killed and another thrown from office. We landed

on the moon. He waited out the war in Germany, playing Army soccer
and rarely writing home. The airline coffee's bitter in its paper cup,
the creamer pasty where the mixer didn't reach. She won't live
until they land. He doesn't know. The airplane cradles its cargo above water
so far and dark it might as well be plate glass.

Genealogy

My father's father was a woodstove. He snapped and roared.

He crackled in the basement. They fed him
so they wouldn't freeze.

Games

When we were children we wanted to be orphans.
The snow came early and halved the treeline.
Branches still flush with leaves heaved with ice and snow
and split at the waist. The sky was then a curtain

lifted on an empty stage. We crawled in the snow
to the back of the yard—past the clothesline taut with ice,
past the barn where the cows stomped their feet in frosted mud.
In the farthest corner of the yard, under the tree

whose bark was ridged so deep we pressed our fingers through
and felt the tree's black heart, we made of snow and fallen limbs
a cave, nestled in to wait for evening. Each branch
was encased in ice, slender tubes we slipped off and held

to the pale evening light. We shivered in our snowsuits,
whispering the story of our parents' death. We imagined
the tragic news, our photogenic weeping, tire tracks
on the gravel drive covered again in snow. But no.

We did not wish. We knew our small thoughts had power,
as when, the winter before, after he told me
your father's gone and won't come back and waited,
thin-lipped, to see me cry, I wished my grandfather dead

and within the year we'd buried him. The days
were slow and edgeless, so we imagined them
torn. This was no game. When the darkness came
and our mother called us over and over, we did not move.

Lent

On Saturdays I drank pilfered liquor,
kissed boys in backseats, in basements

where the parents were always
out of town. Spent Sundays

penitent at mass. The slender
marble aisle. The cracked leather kneeler.

The congregation sitting and standing,
kneeling and sitting in a stuttering unison

as I replayed the rhythm
of hand on——, tongue on——,

my prayer-bent body arched
with aimless lust. I knew.

I had learned in church: to be bodied
was to be sinful. I gave up milk,

gave up spoons, shaved a thumbnail
down to meet its fleshy bed.

Gave up chicken and carved each night
the pan-fried meat from thigh bone,

fork-stabbed the knobby joints. Wished myself
up out of my limbs and aches.

Watched my hipbones rising
like the crescent moon. If this

was wrong, why had they made
Christ's body so beautiful?

He hung there
an object lesson in desire

and its aftermath. I listened.
Christ said, *put your hand here.*

3

Our Wilderness Period

Because we could not love the given world
we left it. Set sail as pilgrims for
a distant shore, though we were not, as they are,
thankful. We knew enough to know what would
await us: water, shore, water, world

without end, Amen. We housed our Lord
in words and ferried him across the waters.
And through that bitter ocean crossing we wept
and prayed with one wind-ragged voice. Our Lord
thrummed fast beneath our tongues. He heard our cries.

And when we reached the shore and saw the scrub
brush and the evergreens beyond, saw first
this wild edgeless land before us, it was then
that I first felt the badness itching in me.

That badness itched at me all summer.
At first we slept fireside, wrapped in wool.
Our men searched the coast for solid new world timber,
then found and felled an entire inland orchard.

They framed us in our houses, blacked the roofs
with old world tar. The bedrooms walls are green.
A rivulet of sap drips from a knot,
and I tongue the joints when mama looks away.

We walk into the woods each morning, shake
the berries from their brambles. Our men hunt
creatures too wild or dumb for fear. These months
are sweet and none of us knows hunger yet.

We have a tender Lord. His words are breadcrumbs.
Each summer dusk we follow their trail home.

Each dusk we trail our mothers home. The men
serve themselves sliced meat splayed on white platters.
The girls spend meals in silent prayer. I pray too,
though I am not good. I cannot hear

the Lord in church. Sister is slim with virtue
and I grow fat. I cannot fast but sneak
the seed potatoes from the cellar, dredge
them raw through fat left in the frying pan.

One Sunday supper when the wives rise
to sing the grace, one cursed childless woman
refuses. Her husband hauls her up. He makes
her say the Lord's Prayer as he beats her down.

Only a wicked woman would rather weep
than bear her man a son. Our mama said.

I was like that, born bad. Mama said so,
after. Come harvest, the girls hear deep within
the night forest the Lord's own voice, calling.

But sister is the only one he touches,
and sometimes that first fall I hear her moaning,
the bodied Lord above her. Mama whistles

and sister grows thick-middled. Soon there is
a baby kicking. The kicking splits her
and then she's thin again, though swollen, bloodied,
the child a wrong-born bundle wrapped tight

in mama's finest sheets. While mama prays
and weeps, the fathers drink the last good whiskey
then dig. Before the first hard frost, they know,
they'll bed sister down in dark and rocky earth.

The girls now sleep with rocks beneath their beds,
and most sleep paired, a charm against the fever.
The day we buried sister our sweet Lord
went under with her. Now that He won't speak

we pray by touch instead. Lust-struck we sit
fireside and palm each other's wondrous bodies,
tongue, sinew, lip, and bone our gospel now.

A wicked hunger grips us. The men
field dress their kill and roast the beasts
on spits kept turning in the churchyard. We strip
the woods of prey and scrape our storehouse bare.

When winter finally finds us, the hunger
holds us still. We suck the marrow from the soup bones.
Our Lord won't speak. Our bellies won't fill.

Because our Lord will still not speak, we gnaw
the armrests from our chairs. Mama burns books
to warm the tips of frost-bit fingers and then
we have no stories left to tell the children.
That stillness grips us. When neighbors pass we leave
their houses open so our missing Lord
may see what He has done. Once He called us
each by name. Now, only hunger and snow.

Some girls still walk, thin-dressed, to church to kneel
and listen for his footsteps, coming back.
I hold a mirror to my fever-mouth
and watch my gums turn black. I was faithful
once. I believed that He would pick me up,
that He would see my sins and wounds and heal them.

I confess: the sins and wounds that bear us down
are mine alone. It was my wickedness
that brought these hardships on us. Nights our Lord
came to visit sister I listened through the wall,
I moaned in rhythm with them. I wanted the Lord
and when I could not have him, wished him gone.

And now we cannot sleep at night for cold.
The men fillet a lone doe felled by disease.
The girls sleep for days, curled together
like filigree. And even now I am

not good. I wander through the empty rooms
and pocket what the dead have left. I stitch
their lockets and their soup spoons in my hem.
I cannot love this Lord. The world, instead.

Before and After, Botched

You made promises.
When I saw the herd of swine
switched to admirers, saw
their flowing locks and cloven
pedicures, I was in
for both a penny and a pound.
All spring I was your little lamb,
held in thrall. You liked me
smaller, fresh-shorn and smelling still
of creekbed and switchgrass. All fall
you gorged on fatback bacon,
pork chops and leafy greens
braised in rendered lard. You turned
your gracious face from all of us. The girls
turned back to swine. The ice and wind
that winter stripped me and I licked
the runoff from the troughs,
gnawed the tender center
from my bed of straw. I believed once
in your prayers and your conversion stories.
I was a fool and am still made of flesh.

Still Life with Mannequin and Leg of Lamb

I am hunger, the breadth and depth of me,
you said, and it was years before I'd learn that you were always
    full of shit. The girls never seemed
like real girls. When you met the sweet young typist
    at a cocktail party and took her home
 it didn't seem like a real death
    because she was sprawled out on the chaise longue
in matching bra and panty like a lingerie model
    or a bargirl after an especially good fuck. Never mind
the puncture marks at neck and thigh, the purpling
    at the wound sites. *We're all still animals,*
you said, *I'm just a more sharp and honest one.*

Fire Plan

At this magnitude, forest fires make their own weather.
We've made our fire plan, the careful list
of what we cannot bear to lose. The train tracks shudder
and buckle. We douse the lawn and wait inside the house.
Bulldozers score the earth to keep the fire
from crossing into town. The tinder of slats and fence posts

flare up. The time to leave has passed,
so we draw the blinds and dream of winter. Weather
turns quickly in drought. I came to learn fire's
bitter grammar, the past-perfect studded with sudden burning. Acreage lost
is the least of it. We watch the porch on the neighbor's house
go up, radiant heat igniting curtains through glass. Our shutters

splinter but do not give. The truck windows shatter.
We hear the fire's howling as a chorus of wolves and wait for it to pass.
The saplings are cords of fire. Inside the house
I count the silver, sort forks and knives, rub tarnish from weathered
creamers and serving dishes. The burnt trees moan as the last
siren whistles out of town. This is what the fire

claims. The house glistens like a monument to fire.
The flames crackle like boots snapping kindling, the stuttering
voice of ruin. After, in the orchard, I scrape charred skin of the last
apple that smells still of apple. The seeds here pass
as metaphor, but we know better. We have survived the weather,
desire's brutal footfalls, the lost years that house

secrets. Bodies found inside burnt houses
leave nothing to bury. So thorough is fire's
blessing sacrament. We have survived. Whether
we learn is another matter. The shops in town stay shuttered.
What was it that you whispered as the fire passed
over us? The burnt fields sing a somber melody, loss

whispering its secret names. This fire will not be the last.
Think of the dead found between car and house.
Think of those who fell, running past,
before we could see them touched by fire.
Then turn your pale face from the shutters.
We are not those dead. We are shapes made by weather.

Frontier Thesis

The wilderness made us strong
so we got wilder. When the storms roar down
we roar them up again. You make a bird's nest from my hair
and use the featherbed for kindling. You make a fortress
from my aprons and slice through all the battlements
to let invaders in. We don't know how we got here
or who we were before but now we're ravenous
like prairie fire. At night we howl like mountain lions.
They love their young like us but their teeth
are more ferocious. When we've eaten the last of our rations
we set fire to the grass to flush the rabbits. When the winter
comes it stays all year.

Rabbit Starvation

In fall we angel in the front lawn,
the fallen leaves turning to powder around us.
I split a squash and roast it with butter and sage,
and in winter we dig the turnips from the root cellar.
With each slice my tongue catches
on my teeth. I boil potatoes pocked and latticed
after I cut their black eyes out. You're a scarecrow
in an argyle sweater, all elbows and moth holes.
I try to dream the harvest back but instead see only
snow that clogs the paths to market,
the rabbits you shoot and skin in the fields.
At night we seashell in our separate frozen beds
and through the snow-bright days, on the lean meat
of your care for me, I starve.

Inventing the Body

1.

She is first a molar
blinking up from rubble
in the Afar Drift.

Her skull is crushed
and shattered. No trees grow

along the wind-scraped
hillside where a world ago
she lay down to die.

Touched, her bones
turn to powder, so the men

jacket her in plaster,
crate and carry
to the capital. They

clean and scan
her bones. They'll
pry from her
all there is
to know.

2.

In the Afar, land
of flash flood, scorpion,
serpent, dust
tornado, unrest,

the sun bleaches fossils the instant
erosion thrusts them up
so that at once the bones
are earth-colored

and the earth is bone-colored.
The men here crawl the earth

because they believe
the first branch

that split us from the animal world
will soon be seen.

3.
Hyoid is the ugly word
for the floating bone
that lets speech
grow. She did not
have one, so she gaped
and roared.

What did she think of,
those long years in the dirt?
Before fire, before
dreams. What thoughts she had
belonged to her alone.

When the words began to stir in her
were they a seedling sprouting
hyena, antelope or a starling
cresting into flight? Did she feel

the tender humming *jumplily, catfish,*
the rapid flare as she lit
on the precise right name?
Peafowl. Kudu. Camellia.

4.
They raised her
with brushes and scalpels,
adhesives and picks.

Teams of men spent
three field seasons collecting
every bone, tooth, snail,
seed, and scrap of fossil wood.
The dark clay of her stratum
streaks the record red.

The men build for her a world
of catfish, hyenas,
doves. They think if they
return the songbirds
and the grassland
she'll learn to speak.

Hackberry, swan fig, kudu.
Terrapin and *tortoise.* The names
pearl up as dust
between her mandible and molar.

5.

Her bones become a body
in their hands. Touched,
she breathes again,

takes shape. The men spend years
drafting and re-drafting
her body, resurrecting
the pelvis and the jointed hips
until they can hold her up

to cameras. This body, too,
a draft. An early and abandoned
version, the awkward walking
that led us to this ground life.

6.

She had not yet
lost the trees. She climbed
through canopy, she gripped and held
with hands shaped like extinction.

She died between volcanoes.
Her body tossed and shifted
until erosion sifted her
sunward.

A long cairn of black stones
marks the hillside where her bones
were pulled from earth. She lived for years
there in the dirt
and when they rose her up again
it changed her.

7.
In reconstruction she bares
her teeth, stares across
an unfound shoulder.

A single vertebra
turned sideways
stands in for
the slender river
of her spine.

The tibia and ulna. The cracked
and jagged femur. They cannot
put her back entirely. Her story rises
like woodsmoke
from these fractures.

4

Bad Magic

It starts out simple, with blindfolds
and sleights of hand. I'll be the girl
you practice on, I'll let you
pull a nest of ravens from my hair
then saw me open on your mother's couch.
I'm very still.
    At the reservoir, when
you strip and handcuff me
for the underwater escape
I won't squirm or make a sound.
        But after a time I tire
of your illusions. I want
real tricks, the kind that hurt, or none at all.
    For your final act you stitch
the raven's feathers to my skin, right through
my favorite sequined dress. You stroke the soft down
beneath the shoulder strap but when my hands
turn to talons you won't let me touch you
in any of the ways you've taught. I bring back
carrion for your breakfast, I preen
and squawk and still you will not have me.
    Fool magician. I was such a good
girl. Now I'll have your heart.
Before the curtain falls and I crest off
I'll pluck it from your chest
like a rabbit from a hat.

We Won't Make it to the Talkies

The bad man lashed me to the tracks,
then laughed. The front row ladies gasped
as, in the paper distance, between
the painted hills, a freight train

suddenly appeared. You rescued me
on horseback and we galloped off
unharmed, hooves kicking a confetti
of dust across imitation desert.

When the time arrived to kiss
we danced. I swooned on cue. You wooed
by rote. I knew that you romanced
me for the camera only. Still I felt

your palm raise heat across my back
as we tapped through our final dance.
The words we never spoke just flashed
across the screen. The silences

I felt for you unhorsed me, love,
and then you left. I called for you
but couldn't hear my voice above
applause. The pianist played us out.

Vigil

I was good for you. I was on
my best behavior, I was on my knees
whole afternoons, scrubbing the linoleum
until Pine-Sol and ammonia blurred my vision.
I sat nights on the front stoop, ankles crossed,
watching as one by one the other driveways
claimed their husbands. Because you taught that faith
is not the same as vision, I waited in the foyer
in the dark. I waited. I rehearsed the role
of good and faithful wife, even in your absence,
even while no one watched. I swapped
the decorative guest soaps in the powder room
when the sunlight faded them from peach to beige.
I breaded chicken cutlets and fried them in oil
so hot I could nearly see my own face in the skillet.
I turned all the mirrors to the wall. I have lived
this dollhouse life for years, each Thursday washing
your unworn undershirts and hanging them on the line,
each Sunday ironing your slacks. I'd do anything
to work the magic of your coming back.

Friendly Letter

My Love,

    my Frankenstein, I made you up. I built a model lover
from the scrap heap at the neighbor's curb on trash day,
the tin cans, shattered side tables, scavenged bits not yet
ravaged by raccoons. Do you remember how I wanted the moon?
I swallowed it in secret, the night we sat on your front lawn
in a silent feud. I cast your scapula into the woods and sent
the dog careening after it to train him on your scent. I like you better
like this. I tied a bow around your sutured joints and called them
elbow, solar plexus, kneecap. Discretion, darling, is the better part
but still I long to hear you speak. When you loved me
you called me on the telephone. Now I stitch a voice box
from cable and string. When I can figure out this radio,
its glitchy dials and rusted-out switches, I'll make you sing.

Horses Dream of Horses

My Darling Z, My Feverlily—

May I call you
    Dearest, may I speak to you
as *sweetheart*, *sugar lump*, the *honeyed*

    apple of my—When we first met
you were a gin-swilling art school darling.
    When you leaned across the bar to order

I saw the milk-white flesh
    below your collarbones, the freckles
shadowboxed by breasts and blouse.

    Saw the careful way he wasn't looking.
He did not love me then. I know. I was just
    a body then, skeleton held

by whipstitch and slipknot, just synapse, firing
    and firing. He was a boy, had fingers
that prodded and opened. Warm body

    on the lawn, scapular on the bedstand.
I knew he'd love you better and by year's end
    I was right. He left

and I was *I* again—
    a ridged and ridden hillside.
But pardon me. I speak too long

and sit too close. I spent a long year
   in the earth, I made you
in my image. I have traveled back

   to hear if only once
your voice, to see
   the full-moon glint of your incisors.

All Good Girls Deserve

My Dearest Miss Z—

I know you, dear. Have seen you
    standing on your porch each evening,
backlit by starlight. I know the year

    you thinned to bone. The way all good girls do.
I know the blade, the rhythm as it strips
    and hones, how the body petals up

obedient beneath its weight.
    I would like to hold your wrist
to flame, to see the blue veins lit

    by the candle's pulsing heart, the arterial thumping.
I would like to tell you
    how he held me down, how I said only

deeper. His name a sore
    I can't stop tonguing. You have said that I
should be ashamed, but I have words

    for you. I was not raised for this. To be
the other. My mother taught the salad fork,
    the polished silver, the body's openings

named in a hush. That a good girl
    crosses at the ankles. That a lady shows herself
by the foot's high arch. I was a girl once,

too. I wanted the wound.

Fervent Missive

Sir—

I have kept my secrets. And been stuffed with them, as on the county's
goose day. I tell no one how at night you came to me and slipped your hand

between my ribs, how then I knew no heart was left beating
in my chest. After, another boy touched me and all at once my skin

had edges. I was that docile once. I loved you with my girl-heart, the false
one that like a baby tooth lost its root and fell away. I know the irises

won't bloom this year. Here, the dead
stay dead. Once I trusted that when the time was right

you would teach me when and how to leave you. I see now
that in this matter, as in so many others, I have been forsaken.

Revisionist Love Story

My Darling Z——

Though you have not asked,
    I will try again to say
what happened. He left me

    in a rented farmhouse. The cows
passed long days lowing in the far fields,
    the hides of Holsteins dappled

like a Rorschach. Once I saw
    a horseshoe and once a pitchfork.
In those early scooped-out days

    I was ravenous. I stripped the green beans
from their vines, fried bacon
    in a blackened skillet. When the farmer's sons

left on the porch steps fresh-bottled milk, warm
    and smelling still of back field hay
I gulped it down. And then my body

    said no. Because I could not eat
I settled in to plan for winter.
    I raised the piglets mean and cooed

when they snapped my feeding hands.
    I harvested habaneros and scotch bonnets,
lined them on the counter

like plucked molars. I cleaned and canned them
barehanded, filled the mason jars
   with their flesh and syrup, held them in the boiling water

until the seals slurped shut. After,
   blisters rose around my nailbeds like the harvest moon.

Birds Keep Nothing in Their Bones

My Dear Miss Z——

I have been made a fool of.
      The far wind harrows me: these limb-stripped
voices, this ghost pipe, a hymnal

      lined with splintered bone.
Years I thought he'd be my story's end
      and he was not. Pity me these indiscretions,

my simpering. He thinks only
      of your slivered tongue, your thighs.
When the final bird was served

      I ate it all and left the rest for scrap.
These bones have not yet
      whitened to your taste. You demand patella,

clavicle, a toothsome ankle. A child's milk molar
      rooted still to jaw. I would like to bend before you,
brush your hair. I offer up this flayed skin,

      a hyphenated strip. Your fair hair
a hieroglyph. Your face a bitter white,
      the bitten cuticle pinking.

Pity me these long lost wishes.
      When night sails down the howling
is dreadful. You say there is no thing like death

but I have been bent and entered
by prayer and if this is not
    death's slender walking—

Unsent Defense

Sir—

I do not care for you. The long vowels say their names and I am the voice
sealed under glass. I am the burnt terrarium, its corners smoke-dark. Christ

wants us to be hot-hearted. She—your sweetheart, your sometime darling —
has my name. She has the letters, the porch door, the key hid

under rock. She knows the misread book, the missed sacrament. She has
my name and she has sworn to speak it to the town. As you have said, *better*

to marry than to burn and I am no one's wife. She will say
that I deserve this. I know only what I said. And what I did—I did.

Cutting Nature at the Joint

My Hothouse Flower, My Dearest Z—

Even in the black heart of this new year
   the sky is a slapped before-storm blue
that hides the cold the way

   you hide your tongue behind your teeth.
When I wake I watch my breath above
   the moth-gnawed blankets.

This house's every joint is drafty. I feel the palm of winter
   on me always, its lewd breath in my face.
I have tried to tell you something of my mind.

   There is in nature
no place to cut and not
   take meat and tendon too.

Small cuts bloom on the body, inexplicable
   as house fire. I am your twinned
and riven countryside. You are the slim-limbed

   chestnut. I know you
through this fixed diction, this fastened warbling
   He had words that lived for years

beneath my skin. No use now
   trying to say what happened or why or how.

Come Fetch

I was the worst of all possible
wives. I married the wrong man
and followed him home. I slept
at his feet, I begged at his table

for scraps. These were the beds
we'd made and so we lay there, stiff
and soundless. And some nights
he moved above me joylessly

then left to wash and sleep
in other beds, wrapped in other
blankets. Days I wandered
through his many-chambered

heart and inside every empty room
I found a cabinet, locked. I didn't need
the key. I knew whose slender
untouched body I would see inside, knew

I'd find her facedown, smudged with earth
because a man like him will do that
when he loves. I pawed her
up again, I nosed the dulcet

rot of her, the savory flesh
of thighs and ass. I saw that she
looked nothing like me, not even
in the moss and rigor mortis of her afterlife

apparel. I loved him then. I gripped
her by the ankle and dragged her
to the hearth. I brought both our bodies
back for proof.

The Secret Nancy

THE DARK AND HANDSOME STRANGER MYSTERY
He's been trailing her all over town. She hears
him just behind her on the sidewalk
walking home. She feels him watching
as she scrapes the dishes clean. She can hear
the ghosts behind her writing. Nancy reads
the local papers, checks with all her sources.
No one's missing. No poisoned swooning
debutantes, no jewel thieves at the Mayor's
inaugural soirée. Nancy presses
her face to the glass. He's standing in her yard.

THE CLUE AT THE ABANDONED DRIVE-IN
She doesn't know his name. The ghosts won't write
but urge her back to town, toward
a volunteer job at the local library,
toward spying on a new and suspect
neighbor, Miss McDonald. Nancy knows
good girls wear gloves to drive
and wash the dishes, wear slips and stockings
under summer dresses. She won't. She's off the plot.
Her stranger never smiles, never speaks. She feels
his eyes on her as she undresses.

THE SIGN OF THE BURNT-OUT STREETLAMP
Ned always was a timid thing, daring only
once to graze her thigh when Father
glanced away. But this man has hands. He finds her
as she's sleuthing and under lamplight fingers
her silk slip's ribboned hem. She's ready

for bed. He's below her window, waiting,
her flashlight the beacon blinking *yes*,
blinking *come*. And when he mounts her trellis
and enters her window, when he lifts her nightdress—
she won't say no, won't be sorry.

ACKNOWLEDGEMENTS

With thanks and appreciation for the many people who made this book possible.

Many, many thanks to the teachers whose time and attention has shaped this work: Quan Barry, Amaud Jamaul Johnson, Jesse Lee Kercheval, Ronald Wallace, Jan Beatty, Lynn Emanuel, Jeff Oaks, Anthony Petrosky, Darin Cicotelli, and especially Sharon McDermott, whose care and generosity stun me still. Thanks also to Jim Brown, Christa Olson, and Morris Young, who have helped me to see the scholarly and creative parts of my work as happening in concert. With appreciation also for the institutions that have supported my development as a writer, particularly the University of Wisconsin-Madison's MFA program and the University of Pittsburgh's undergraduate Writing Program.

This book is better for the careful reading and incisive feedback of several friends: Erinn Batykefer, Lauren Berry, Brittany Cavallaro, Rebecca Dunham, Rebecca Hazelton, Cynthia Marie Hoffman, Josh Kalscheur, Jacques Rancourt, Rita Mae Reese, Casey Thayer, and Angela Voras-Hills. And Heather Bowlan, my first best reader.

Heartfelt gratitude to Alex Lemon for selecting this book and to the National Poetry Series and Milkweed Editions for supporting its publication.

With love to my family, particularly my parents, Marilyn and Larry Seigh and Doug and Ellen Reddy, for their unwavering support.

For Smith, always.

Grateful acknowledgement to the editors of the following journals, where poems from this collection first appeared.

Anti —: "The Case of the Double Jinx"
Barn Owl Review: "Still Life with Mannequin and Leg of Lamb"
Boxcar Poetry Review: "Fervent Missive"
Cimmaron Review: "Portrait of My Father as a Young Man with a Bludgeon"
Fail Better: "Before and After, Botched," "Rabbit Starvation," "We Won't
    Make it to the Talkies," "Come Fetch"
Going Down Swinging (Australia): "Lent"
Indiana Review: "Big Valley's Last Surviving Beauty Queen"
Linebreak: "Horses Dream of Horses," "Games"
Memorious: "Lent"
Smartish Pace: "Divine and Mechanical Bodies"
The Collagist: "Lucy in Chrysalis"
The Journal: "All Good Girls Deserve," "Birds Keep Nothing in Their
    Bones," "Family Portrait with Rosary and Steak Knife"
Tupelo Quarterly: "Ex Machina," "Friendly Letter," "Why the McKean
    County Lifeguards Left Town," "Bad Magic," "A Theory of Disaster"

"My Girlhood Apothecary" also appeared in *Best New Poets 2011*.
"The Case of the Double Jinx" also appeared in *The Best of the Net 2011*.
"Divine and Mechanical Bodies" also appeared in *New Poetry from the Mid-
    west 2014*.

"Inventing the Body" was inspired by the discovery of *Ardipithecus ramidus*,
    who at 4.4 million years old is the earliest known hominid. The Octo-
    ber 2009 *Science* reports on this finding.

Nancy Reddy's poems have been published in *32 Poems*, *Tupelo Quarterly*, and *Best New Poets of 2011* (selected by D.A. Powell), with poems forthcoming in *Post Road* and *New Poetry from the Midwest*. She holds an M.F.A. and PhD in composition and rhetoric from the University of Wisconsin. She is Assistant Professor of Writing and First Year Studies at Stockton University in southern New Jersey.